GOD IS THIS A MAN MY GOD IS THIS A MAN MY GOD IS THIS A MAN

Cover image by Alessandro Guttenberg
Cover and book design by Rob Arnold and Rebecca Wolff

Published in the United States by Fence Books
Science Library, 320 University at Albany
1400 Washington Avenue, Albany, NY 12222

www.fenceportal.org

Fence Books are printed in Canada by The Prolific Group and
distributed by Small Press Distribution and Consortium Book Sales
and Distribution.

Library of Congress Cataloguing in Publication Data
Sims, Laura [1973-]
My god is this a man/Laura Sims

Library of Congress Control Number: 2014932376

ISBN 13: 978-1-934200-73-5

First Edition
10 9 8 7 6 5 4 3 2

Fence Books are published in partnership with the University at
Albany and the New York State Writers Institute, and with invaluable
support from the New York State Council on the Arts and the National
Endowment for the Arts.

MY GOD IS THIS A MAN   MY GOD IS

A MAN *MY GOD IS THIS A MAN MY GOD IS THIS A MAN MY GOD IS THIS A MAN*

LAURA SIMS

FENCE
BOOKS

albany, new york

Acknowledgments

Many thanks to the editors of the following journals, in which poems (or former versions of poems, in many cases) from *My god is this a man* first appeared: *A Sing Economy, Aufgabe, CAB/NET, Cannot Exist, Colorado Review, Denver Quarterly, Parthenon West Review, Ping Pong, Raleigh Quarterly, Seven Corners,* and *Trickhouse.*

Thanks also to Dexterity Press and Answer Tag Press for designing and publishing a handsome broadside of the poem formerly titled, "My god is this a man."

And my deepest thanks, as ever, to Rebecca Wolff.

For you

I am here

I have always

been here

I rode around and rode around

the middle

of the world

I cleaned myself   a bottle and inside

                    she fell

on top of me

Shocked, the human beings

I lied her on the floor

I said, "I lied her on the floor"

I don't
I don't deny (I wasn't there) but

I'd had the dearest little dream

I was good — or good enough — and careful

It was — both — fell backward on the bed

and she

became

a woman

being

done to

See the pines

that are

"such as they are"

and the ones that escaped

There were horrors

then horrors

were stacked onto those

I vanished into the park

The pure, blank thought
the fresh soil
the wilderness

gathered a
pile of stones

In the
marble
halls

I'm controlled, I am not
doing
interviews. Still

(Defendant nods affirmatively.)

I note the defendant has nodded affirmatively.

Let the record reflect

the defendant

has nodded assent

I felt

the low sound

when I   stepped   around the island

Only the rifle could touch us both and the glass jug

shuddered in the earth

She rose

and went to the window

What swung

from the rafters, soft —

The hordes

of the curious

Yellow Cord – a Golden Earring – and a Surge

Lit me up and led me

to the center of

the quiet & unmeaning

shadow of the Gator Bowl —

The mind, erased,

became

     a million thin veneers — a snake — a feast of plastic forms — a giant

ruling twilight, making

riot in the earth and I

endured a spasm and began

As I wavered behind him

I called him myself

TRUST

had been

hammered

out of me

His face

shone
at dusk

so odd

yet so pleasing. When he caught me his fevered embrace

——————————Fire trucks

mask the sound————————

He was Everywhere

                (hurting)

The Nothing

Like Thought

                (scattered expertly)

                (missed)

His Big Heart

                (a can of wet lard)

                (all the same)

His Deeds

                (would not)

                (stop him from reaching)

The Stupid

Free World

The defendant says

nothing and

yes a thousand times yes

a million times

yes

Out of a vacuum & into

I

That heavenly

structure – the world – there

everything matters

II

At a feast

made of beautiful feelings

you learn

the other must serve you

III

And suffer

you suffer

yourself to observe

I stood

like a rag from which the
soul

escaped

"For heavens / sake catch me / before I kill more / I cannot control myself." – Bill Heirens

I
Control

Heavens
I

Cannot
Catch

More

Before
Heavens

For
Heavens

Sake
Heavens

I
Kill
For

"I do not know why I did that. That was something, I do not know why. I do not know why it was done." – Bill Heirens

Why
Something

I did
Did I

Something
Was done

I
Know

Why
Do not

Know
It was done

"You get inside the other person and the other person gets inside you." - Bill Heirens

And
The

Get
You

Inside
Person

Gets
Other

You
You

Get
Other

Inside
Inside

You

"In plain words I think I am a worm."

- Bill Heirens

I
Think

Words
Am I

In
I Think

A
I think

Worm
I

Think
Am

I think
Words

I think
Worm

"It wasn't as dark and scary as it sounds. I had a lot of fun…killing somebody's a funny experience." – Albert deSalvo

It was
Somebody's

Fun
A dark

Lot
Funny

Sounds
(Funny-

Scary)
And

Somebody
Killing

Experience

I remember the hammer

WHO

Ransacked

the room. The words:

No Thrill, and No Happiness

The body knows just

what to do. Let the record reflect

each breath, each rib

each bone letting go

Murder son(g)

I am nothing!
— Kip Kinkel

I plan to live in a big black hole

My heart is in the hole

It is gray

"My guns, they blast right through me with a good clean love"

"My guns, they never stabbed me in the back"

Walk into a pep rally with guns.

Walk into a Costco with guns. Walk into a coffee shop with guns. Walk into a party store with guns. Walk into a wedding shower with guns. Walk into a weight room with guns.

Walk into a living room with guns and say

                        All I want is something small.

Settle down, settle down

It's all right, it's all right

Settle down, settle down

It's all right, it's all right

Walk out of a forest with guns. Walk into a pasture with guns. Walk into a valley with guns. Walk into shadows with guns. Walk into late afternoon sunlight with guns. Walk into the house with guns. Walk upstairs with guns. Walk into the attic with guns. Walk out the window with guns. Walk into air with guns. Walk into paradise with guns and say

Oh God ... I am

always alone

Settle down, settle down, etc.

Something

warm

on my arm —

it was

Wears
holes
around
my neck

&

I cast him down

in that outhouse

I looked

from

eyeholes

at the

human race

One side was heavily armored

The other side wore   a soft body

                    and ended its days on the grass, beside

the dark footpath

Let the scalp the forehead the shoulders & backs
of the knees

soften. The lower jaw softens away and the mouth

hangs tenderly open

G.R.

I.

Why are some in the river and some

Had old scars

[One head] [Rope marks: hands ankles neck]
[Stone in significant orifice] [Torn corners of mouths]

Was it *what* or *who* they were *day* or *night* was the odor she wore

Above ground

I had a head, but I lost it.

II.

I had a head, but I lost it

III.

The real estate man is one man

The realest man is one man

The real isn't man is one man

The real is man is one man

IV.

What man

V.

You work for me or nobody

Your word for me is nobody

You work me or nobody

You were me or nobody

You were me you were nobody

You worm, you nobody

VI.

When she stood in the darkened gym, the glitter ball

Turned: I knew

A significant woman

Rooted to him, she spoke but her mouth

Don't worry I'm just thrown away

Watery drops

of blood on the dirt, or

Drops of blood

on the dirty water

She wore a good shape,
'she was good in all ways'

There will be more dirt,
more money, no dirty talk

No more nutrition.

Dangling limbs

The downward spiral

The lifeboat

nailed

to the rose-colored wall

Let the eyes settle back

In the head

Let the long bones settle down into the bed

I dreamed a bottle

hanging upside down:

a body goes

over the precipice

Under debris   On Mt. Solo   Snagged on the banks of a creek

Off a logging road   Down a ravine   Lomas de Poleo

The Dumpster next door   Otter Lake   or   The sea floor

The plains of   The desert   or out in   in any case

There

*

When we woke   a whole planet of waste

The spaceships above them

like stars

They fell

to pieces

Hands in one country, heads in another, organs, arms

They wanted their bodies to be handled boldly, as they'd boldly handled

the bodies

on water or land

They carried

their fear of the living, assured

into crawlspaces lighted

with singular bulbs

The gloved police
seemed nearly human once.

Or is it *early*?

The gloved police seemed early human once.
They pried up all the floorboards in the house.

The State unearthed a tiny

wooden door. And paint.
They witnessed "red
upon the Hoosier moon"

and hit all fours and combed the fields

for days

shoulder to shoulder, through the waving stalks and small debris

They found your finished Myth. They tore it up

There is warmth in the palms. Or coolness in the palms.
There is

nothing you need and no right

way to feel

In a field in a

field in a field in a field in a field in a
field in a field in a field in a field in a
field in a field in a field in a field in a
field in a field in a field in a field in a
field in a field in a field in a field in a
field in a field in a field in a field in a
field   in a field in a field in a
field   a body in a field in a field in a
field   in a field in a field in a
field in a field in a field in a field in a
field in a field in a field in a field in a
field in a field in a field in a field in a

body sparkled in a diamond field
body dampened a fire field body
clamored in a nation field body
tumbled in a battle field body
spent in a cash field body greased
in a rifle field body caught in a
force field body ends in a body
field

We found a body in a burned field.

Now a wet field. A sooty field. A

wet-because-it's-dawn field. What is

also a mine field. And is often a

playing field. Once any but a body

field.

He feels
a body is a   somebody

She feels
a body is a   nobody

They feel   with their soles
or knees or bare feet or palms or
sharpened sticks

                  and the body

        softly

      responds

as a body in a field

is a body is a body is a body is a body
is a body is a body is a body is a body
is a

field

Author's Note

In writing this book, I read the confessions, interviews, letters and journal entries of, with, and by convicted (or suspected) murderers David Berkowitz, Robert Browne, Richard Trenton Chase, Jeffrey Dahmer, Albert DeSalvo, Albert Fish, Robin Gecht, Ed Gein, David Gore, Ricky Javon Gray, Belle Gunness, Bill Heirens, J. Frank Hickey, Kip Kinkel, Bobby Joe Long, Henry Lee Lucas, Pauline Parker, Colin Pitchfork, Gary Ridgway, Myrtle Schaude, Edward Spreitzer, Dzhokhar Tsarnaev, Jack Unterweger, Aileen Wuornos and the (still unknown) Zodiac Killer. I have sometimes used words, phrases, images, or ideas from these sources in the poems.

The writing on the black pages is a mix of the language from Dzhokhar Tsarnaev's bedside confession just following the Boston Marathon bombings and my "Bedtime Relaxation" meditation mp3 available at: medweb.mit.edu.

Books by Laura Sims

My god is this a man
Stranger
Practice, Restraint
(winner of the Alberta Prize)

Fare Forward: Letters from David Markson
(powerHouse Books)